ISBN: 978-82-93697-21-3

- Successful Dating -

No More Frogs
ARIES

21 March – 20 April

by
Cathrine Dahl

CONTENTS

- Successful Dating -
No More Frogs

by Cathrine Dahl

No More Frogs - Successful Dating is your one-stop dating guide. No unnecessary blah-blah. The information is right here, at your fingertips.

This guide can be used in several ways. It's a handy tool when you want to prepare yourself a little. It can give you an advantage when going on a date or getting to know someone you've just met - or even someone you've known for a while.

Although this guide can help you angle your approach, remember to be true to yourself. Have fun, be wise, follow your heart - and keep your feet on the ground!

- Cathrine Dahl

Preface:
A few words about compatibility, and why compatibility guides can give you the wrong idea.

So you've met this Gemini you really, really like, but you're a Scorpio, and the compatibility guides say you're a lousy match. Guess what? That's rubbish!

Some compatibility guides offer a very simplistic approach, claiming that your best matches are the star signs within the same element as you:

Fire: Aries, Leo and Sagittarius
Earth: Taurus, Virgo and Capricorn
Air: Gemini, Libra and Aquarius
Water: Cancer, Scorpio and Pisces

Other guides are slightly more specific, declaring that we are compatible with star signs within our astrological polarity.

Yin: Taurus, Virgo, Capricorn, Cancer, Scorpio and Pisces
Yang: Aries, Leo, Sagittarius, Gemini, Libra and Aquarius

Doesn't look too good, does it? The most optimistic approach has removed half of the population from your dating pool. It doesn't make any sense. The true picture is far more promising...

One star sign, two very different personalities

Each of us has a unique astrological thumbprint determined by the sun, the moon and the planets. The most important factors being your ascending star (ascendant), the sun (star sign) and the moon (feelings).

Let's make it simple

Imagine your star sign being a melody. All the other aspects (the unique positioning of the moon and the planets) are sound effects, applied by a producer with a mixer.

The combination of rhythm, depth and base creates your unique sound. Another person with the same star sign will get his own sound mix and end up with a different beat.

Your personal melody can create wonderful harmonies with star signs you're not supposed to get on with – and nothing but noise with signs that are meant to be matches. You won't find out until you get to know each other.

Let's get to know your date...

THE MALE

YOUR DATE: ARIES
21 March–20 April

The Essence of him

Restless – dynamic – aggressive – impulsive – makes things happen – has a boyish charm; can be slightly childish – energetic – jealous – generous – absent-minded – kind – temperamental – clever – social – has a good sense of humour – confident – passionate – determined – a creative lover – disorganised – masculine – exciting – adventurous – insecure – inspiring

...and remember: This man is not into mind games. Don't tease him or play hard to get. If you do, he'll move on to someone who demonstrates her interest more clearly.

Blind Date – speedy essentials

Who's waiting for you?

You'll probably hear him before you see him. Follow the cheerful laughter, and you'll find your date. Shy? Self-conscious? Not this guy. He's social, and talking to strangers is completely natural to him. He approaches the world with a childlike enthusiasm and curiosity; he's really a kid at heart, and there will always be something naïve and boyish about him, no matter how old he gets. As far as style is concerned, he prefers to be comfortable – but he can impress with a sharp outfit when the situation calls for it. There's no room for snobbery in his laid-back world.

Emergency fixes for embarrassing pauses

The Aries man will start the conversation. If you show him you're interested by feeding him comments and questions, he'll keep it going, and time will fly by. Mr Aries enjoys smart and intelligent women, so don't be afraid to introduce some of your own views and ideas. But don't overreach in an attempt to impress him. This guy can spot a fake quickly. You're either genuine, or you're out. Don't worry if he brings up at topic you know nothing about. Admit any gaps in knowledge, but show interest and ask some questions. He'll appreciate that.

Your place or mine?

Anyplace, really... This is an impulsive guy. Add a dose of adventure and passion, and you'll have a firework on your hands. If the chemistry is right – which is very important – then he won't need much encouragement. He doesn't like wasting his time, so don't give the impression that you're hot if you're not.

Checklist, before you dash out to meet him:

Have some fun ideas of what to eat, drink or do

(hint: be creative)

Wear a nice, casual outfit

(hint: be prepared for different venues)

Show him a photo of you in a fun place or doing something active

(hint: be interesting)

Invite him to a new boutique gym, or something similar

(hint: introduce him to something different)

Have an open mind and be positive

(hint: play along and inspire him)

Tip: This masculine, positive and enthusiastic guy can get surprisingly jealous. Be sparkling, feminine and fun, but avoid flirting with the waiter or bartender – or any guy at all.

CHAPTER 1

PREPARE YOURSELF

Catch his eye, capture his attention
Top 10 attention grabbers

1. Be cheerful and sparkling.
2. Pay attention to your looks. Emphasise your feminine – and sassy – sides.
3. Signal your interest, but don't be obvious.
4. Don't be afraid to show him your independent side.
5. Take the initiative, but without coming on too strong. He is good at picking up hints.
6. Be playful and adventurous – the one in the crowd who's up for trying out that new drink, meal, activity, etc.
7. Don't be eager to please. Be yourself.
8. Be hot, but be cool about it.
9. Admire and respect his masculinity, but give a little resistance.
10. Show interest in his experiences and topics of conversation.

The SHE. The woman!

An Aries man can be pretty flexible when it comes to picking a playmate for the night. On the other hand, choosing a romantic partner requires thorough attention. He expects her to be just as impulsive and enthusiastic as he is. He prefers a sporty and active woman, but she won't get far with him unless she's also classy, sassy and feminine. She must be someone he can be proud of, both in terms of looks and personality. He will lose interest if she doesn't live up to his expectations. Although he enjoys independent women, she must never challenge his masculinity.

The Essence of her
Sporty – active – feminine – has a good sense of humour - confident – charming – independent – loyal – attentive – sassy – entertaining – outgoing – can manage the fine art of charming other men without flirting – curious– loves experiencing new things – enthusiastic – impulsive – open-minded – both seeks and takes regular advice – flexible – not fussy about details – smart – has a twinkle in her eyes – positive – engaging

Aries arousal meter
From 0 to 100... In ten minutes, or less. This is a passionate and erotic guy, and he's pretty flexible about where and when. Why waste time when the mood is right...?

Remember: Be true to yourself

It doesn't matter if he is the most stunning guy you've ever met – if you don't match, you don't match. You may be able to put on a show for a while to hold his attention, but what's the point? We can't please everybody. We all have different needs, dreams, tastes and preferences. There's no such thing as a one-size-fits-all lover. Be yourself, and be true to who you are – always!

Very important: Pay attention to what you say. If you manage to make him think and inspire him, you will ignite a spark in his eyes. Focus on unusual topics. Surf the net before you meet him, and gather stories with an edge.

CHAPTER 2

THE FIRST DATE

Getting your foot in the door
The basics

Whatever you are, be real. The Aries man doesn't fall for the innocent-little-girl vibe. There's a difference between being a little shy and pretending to be coy – and it's the pretending he doesn't like.

Ease into it. It's easy to relax in his company. He will take the initiative, and then it's up to you to tag along. It's like adding wood to a fire – you just have to stoke it to make sure it keeps burning.

Inspire. Introducing him to something new is a good way to pique his interest. Show him your fun, feminine and independent sides. Let him know you're not afraid to stand on your own two feet.

Cherish the masculinity. Tell him about your ideas and ask for his opinion. This is a subtle way to appeal to his masculinity.

Keep it smart and simple. If you spark his creativity and impulsiveness, the two of you may end up in all sorts of unusual places, so dress accordingly.

Whatever you do...

- **DON'T** flirt with other men when he's around.

- **DON'T** criticise his energy.

- **DON'T** bluff, overreach for compliments or tell him white lies.

- **DON'T** be loud or vulgar.

- **DON'T** put on a show or pretend to be someone you're not.

Remember, If you respond to his invitations with vague answers about needing to check your agenda, he'll be gone before you've opened your phone.

- **DON'T** play hard to get and leave him wondering what's going on.

- **DON'T** be too secretive about yourself.

- **DON'T** tease him in bed.

- **DON'T** be bossy or question his masculinity.

- **DON'T** drape yourself in a negative attitude.

The initial stages are important, but don't think too much. If it's not working out, Mr Aries will probably be the first to dash off.

Signs you're in - or not

If you're in, you'll know. If you've managed to capture his interest, he won't waste time. Getting to know you will be his first priority. He will call or text you – or both. He won't be making suggestions for next week. Prepare yourself for a 'later today' or 'tomorrow around lunch'. You'll continue scoring points with this guy if you can keep up with him and show the same level of enthusiasm. For him, life is an adventure – and it's for living. It can be quite refreshing when a guy says: I really like you. I want to see you now!

If you're not sure, or you think you may have misinterpreted something, a few signals will indicate that you've made a strong impression:

Chances are he will...

- call or text you soon after you've said goodbye
- ask for your opinion
- put projects aside to be with you
- include you in his ideas
- be protective of you and bark at men who give you the eye
- be very focused on you and unusually romantic

Not your type? Making an exit

If the two of you don't hit it off right away, he'll probably notice before you do. His social antennas are strong – especially when it comes to women. While keeping the conversation going and entertaining you with stories, he's simultaneously reading your body language and picking up on subtle cues. If you're not into him, he'll know. He moves on quickly and can even be a little blunt about it. Life is to be lived, not wasted. If you can't provide him with the excitement and adventures he's looking for, he'll hit the road.

However, if you have dazzled him with your charm, beauty and knowledge, he may continue trying to win you over. This is when you'll need to put your foot down. Sure, you could just leave, but things will go more smoothly if you help him decide for himself.

Foolproof exit measures:

These suggestions may seem a little drastic, and they may show you in a bad light – but if you really need an exit, these will get you there:

- Start talking about a new savings account you've set up that allows for no flexibility or extra spending. From now on, every little thing needs to be planned
- Tell him you find no-sex relationship fascinating
- Start giving him 'helpful' hints about everything: how to hold his glass or cutlery, the colours he's wearing, etc.
- Talk about your day in detail, including boring titbits about people he doesn't know
- Give the impression that you know very little about anything, and yawn when he tries to enlighten you
- Get giggly and silly at dinner, even if you've only had a soda

CHAPTER 3

SEX'N STUFF

Seductive moves:
How to get him in the mood:

The Aries man is usually attracted to funny, intelligent and attractive women. However, when it comes to sex, his needs are simpler: he's turned on immediately by women who simply stare at him and say YES. He's a master of body language and knows instinctively when a woman is up for a sexual encounter. In other words, you can't really fake anything with this guy – and that means *anything*! However, a distracted Aries may need a little encouragement at times.

Preferences and erotic nature

An erotic suggestion out of the blue will capture an Aries man's attention. How you're dressed matters less than how you act. Hold back a little, but only for the sake of excitement. As soon as you notice a spark in his eyes, start playing and carefully teasing him. Give him time to respond. Appeal to his masculine personality by allowing him to take the lead. Just remember that the teasing stage won't last long. As soon as you've got him going, he'll be ready to release his passion.

Hitting the right buttons

Although every sign has areas that are more sensitive than others, individual sensitivity may vary quite a bit. Don't go body-blind. Honing in on these erogenous zones and forgetting the rest of him is not a good idea. Use his erogenous zones to create sparks while turning him on, and as a passion booster when it gets heated. Watch his body language – including the most obvious of signs! Open your mind to the sensuality of touch and taste.

Key areas
Face and head

Get it on
Get creative. A slight touch to his head can give him goosebumps all over. There are many opportunities to turn him on. You can do it anytime, anywhere – both at home and in public. What other people may interpret as an innocent sign of affection could actually be a seductive moment.

Arouse him
Touch him gently with the tips of your fingers, brush your lips over his ears, kiss his chin and neck, run your hands through his hair or over his head... Doing any of these softly and slowly will arouse him.

Surprise him

An erotic comment when he least expects it can spark his imagination. Follow it up with another comment a little later, and watch his smile grow. Just make sure you're prepared to follow through if you end up in a place where you can do something about it...

Spice it up

A slight variation on a traditional theme can get you far. Change the setup by getting piles of pillows that you can move around. This will enable you to experience positions from new angles.

Remember: Don't confuse his natural masculinity with dominance. He feels no need to dominate his partner – but he does take great pride in himself as a man and his ability to please his woman.

His expectations

Bring it on! He loves excitement and impulsiveness. Actually, he loves most everything – provided it's not boring.

Make it exciting. Neither time nor place matters to this guy when it comes to sex. He's not an exhibitionist, but a touch of excitement – a change of location, for example – is a sure way to spice things up. He's a perfect partner if you feel the need to shake up your erotic routine.

Keep up the pace. The Aries man approaches sex like he approaches everything in life – with energy, passion and enthusiasm. If you're looking for someone to guide you gently during sex, you'd better look elsewhere.

Be fun, be creative. His erotic mind is flexible, and he is open to suggestions. There's just one catch: he expects the same from you. He may feel disappointed if you don't go along with his ideas. If you ever find yourself in this situation, give him a few suggestions, instead – something you're into.

…and be vocal. Make sure to express your pleasure – this is very important to him.

Release your passion. In short, this is a passionate dream of a man looking for a passionate dream of a woman.

Your sensual preferences
Quiz yourself and find out whether this man is for you.

Where on the scale are you?
1 = Don't agree | 3 = Sure | 5 = Agree!

1. There's no such thing a sexual fulfillment without passion and playfulness.
One a scale for 1 to 5, you are: 1 - 2 - 3- 4 - 5

2. Being open-minded is important for expanding your erotic horizon.
One a scale for 1 to 5, you are: 1 - 2 - 3- 4 - 5

3. Too much foreplay can make sex slow and boring.
One a scale for 1 to 5, you are: 1 - 2 - 3- 4 - 5

4. Expressiveness and communication is important during sex.
One a scale for 1 to 5, you are: 1 - 2 - 3- 4 - 5

Score 15–20: Passionate, adventurous and satisfying. You're on the same level, and it's full steam ahead. Enjoy!
14–10: He may seem a bit too surprising at first, but soon, you'll enjoy exploring his erotic world and broadening your horizons.
9–5: He doesn't mind adjusting his lovemaking – provided his partner plays along.
4 – 1: While you prefer closeness, sensuality and intimacy, he charges ahead on a wave of passion. It could be fun – or it could just be a challenge.

CHAPTER 4

GENERAL STUFF

The big picture

Keep in mind that the characteristics of a Aries may vary quite a bit depending on where within the sign he was born, as well as a wide range of additional astrological factors. But for now, let's stick to the basics. Just remember: don't jump to conclusions as soon as you meet him. Give him room to shine. Get to know the man behind the sign.

His personality: Pros and cons

Pros	Cons
• Makes things happen	• Restless
• Enthusiastic	• Jealous
• Has a good sense of humour	• Absent-minded
• Impulsive	• Temperamental
• Confident	• Childish
• Clever	• Impatient
• Adventurous	• Superficial
• Generous and kind	• Hyperactive
• Passionate	• Arrogant
• Masculine	• Indifferent
• Courageous	• Stubborn
• Inspiring	• Insensitive and thoughtless
• Positive and forthcoming	• Overly ambitious
• Boyish and playful	• Enters fleeting relationships

Tip: How to show romantic interest

Suggest doing things together, and be enthusiastic, positive, assertive – and fun. Avoid being too obvious about your feelings, especially if he hasn't made up his mind about his.

Romantic Vibes

Mr Aries:
The impulsive and adventurous partner

The essence

Determined pursuit. He's just as impulsive in his romantic life as he is in every other aspect. As soon as a woman has captured his interest, the energetic Aries will make a move.

Doesn't waste time. He doesn't waste any time hanging around, contemplating. If he feels he's met the woman, he'll have no second thoughts about entering a relationship. He won't risk missing his chance.

...and sometimes a little hasty. His impulsiveness comes with a slight drawback: he doesn't always take the time to think things through. He could save himself hassle and heartbreak if he didn't always rush into the arms of love.

Opens up. A beautiful, charming and intelligent woman is like a truth serum to him: he simply needs to open up. He'll take her hand and let his emotions flow.

Spontaneous. His affection is real, but will it last? When he jumps into a relationship, he tends to forget the practical details ... like whether she's a good match for him. However, as long as his woman manages to keep up with him, admire him and inspire him, he will prove to be a warm, passionate and loyal partner.

Tip: How to show erotic interest

He can read your body language without even thinking about it, so give him a seductive smile. Think about something sensual as you look at him. Your erotic interest will shine through your eyes.

Erotic Vibrations

Mr Aries:
The passionate and playful lover

The essence

100% passion. Passion is part of who an Aries is. It flows through every cell in his body and gives him energy and enthusiasm. This applies to his erotic life as well.

Determined. He may come on a little strong and give the impression that he wants to have things his way. Don't be discouraged – this is just the passionate streak in him.

Erotically playful. He's aggressive, energetic and restless – and far from a once-a-week-under-the-covers type of guy. He is impatient and may start undressing you before you're inside the house, but he'll never be crude about it. He's simply playful and driven.

Yes! - or - No! When he initiates sex, he wants a straight yes or no. No maybes! Girls who 'need to think about it a little' won't stand a chance with him.

Express yourself. In order to feel completely satisfied, he'll need constant reassurance from you. He wants to know that you're enjoying everything as much as he is.

A new twist. He may not be a master of foreplay, but he's a creative wizard who can turn traditional positions into something new and exciting.

CHAPTER 5

COMPATIBILITY QUIZ

———————————————

Are you banging your head against the wall, or does he unleash your positive potential? Do you provoke him or bring out the best in him? Does he make you throw your arms up in exasperation, or do you feel inspired and complete in his company? Are the two of you headed towards doom or dream? Take the test to find out.

Question 1.
What are the characteristics of your perfect partner?

A. Sensitive, romantic and kind.
B. Ambitious, enthusiastic and social.
C. Intense, sensual and mysterious.

Question 2.
How about you? Which of the following words best describe you?

A. Strong, creative and adventurous.
B. Down to earth, loyal and funny.
C. Dreamy, reflective and introverted.

(cont.)

Question 3.
Do you find it difficult to show your feelings?

A. No, not at all. I can talk easily about my emotions.
B. It's not that I find it difficult. I just don't see the point in rattling on about feelings all the time.
C. Sometimes, if I'm worried about not being taken seriously.

Question 4.
What would you do to show affection for your partner?

A. I'd make him a great dinner and treat him to a sensual bath later in the evening.
B. I'd take a day off and do things he finds interesting – even though I might find them a bit boring.
C. I'd buy him an expensive shirt.

Question 5.
Do you prefer to hang out with your old friends, or do you enjoy meeting new people?

A. I like hanging out with people I know well.
B. I love meeting new people – especially people who have different experiences than I do.
C. I don't mind meeting new people, but it's not especially important to me.

Question 6.
How do you feel about living for the moment and having a relaxed attitude towards budgets and finances?

A. That's not my style at all. I need financial security.
B. If you want to live in the moment, you have to spend in the moment!
C. It doesn't have to be either-or. You can be impulsive while still being financially responsible.

Question 7.
Do you enjoy a partner who is passionate and assertive in bed?

A. Yes. Sensitive little kittens are not my style.
B. Not really – too much assertiveness can ruin the emotion and reduce sex to physical workout.
C. Sure, but not every night. Closeness and tenderness are just as important.

Question 8.
Would you ever withhold sex from your partner if you were upset with him?

A. I don't like playing games. If he upset me, I'd tell him straightforwardly.
B. Yes. That's a sure way to get the message through.
C. Never. Sex is something beautiful between two people – not something you trade and bargain with.

Question 9.
What's your approach to showing interest for a guy?

A. I'd shower him with compliments, even if I don't mean half of them.
B. I'd be lively and sparkling while letting him know that I'm up-to-date on what's going on in the world.
C. I'd make it clear that I appreciate strong and adventurous men.

Question 10.
Would you describe yourself as impulsive?

A. Hmm ... not really. Planning is more my thing.
B. I can be impulsive, provided I don't need to make big decisions.
C. Absolutely. Impulsiveness can turn a grey day into an adventure.

SCORE	A	B	C
Question 1	1	10	5
Question 2	10	5	1
Question 3	10	5	1
Question 4	5	10	1
Question 5	1	10	5
Question 6	1	5	10
Question 7	10	1	5
Question 8	5	1	10
Question 9	1	10	5
Question 10	1	5	10

75 – 100

Talk about getting it right. With Mr Aries by your side, all 'life's pieces seem to fall into place. There will be excitement, positive energy, fun challenges, love and passionate sex. What else could you possibly want? You know exactly how to treat your partner to bring out the best in him – and he will reward you with all sorts of pleasures. Maybe most importantly of all, you help him organise his life so he doesn't have to worry about the details that pile up and get in his way.

51 – 74

One thing is certain: you'll never be bored with this guy. Sure, there may be discussions and even some fierce arguments, but that's just the price you pay for passion. The occasional thunderstorm will pass quickly, and you'll probably enjoy good make-up sex. You both enjoy the fact that you can speak freely with each other and never hide your feelings. You can talk to him about anything, even erotic fantasies, without feeling restricted or shy, and he appreciates your frankness. The openness in your relationship allows you to build trust and clear the air when necessary. Although he may come across as a dream, don't let him take over your life completely. He appreciates a woman who can put her foot down and give him a little resistance. Yes, he can be a little demanding at times, but for the right woman, he's a catch.

26 – 50

You're not quite sure what to make of him sometimes. Is he just a big kid with loads of charm and energy – or a childish man who needs to grow up? Don't expect him to mature overnight. The evolution of Mr Aries is a lifelong process. Some women find it fascinating and exciting; others get stressed and frustrated. If you really like him, give him a chance. Ignore the impulses that make him do things out of the blue. If you feel he's about to lose touch with reality, bring him gently down to earth. Don't fuss. You'll achieve more by being supportive and enthusiastic. But when you get tired of being a cheerleader, let him know. Tell him what you would like to do. This can actually produce positive results. This guy would prefer his woman to speak his mind, not just grumble in the background. Besides, he wants you to enjoy life as much as he does.

10 – 25

Think about it for a moment: is it possible you've confused excitement with compatibility? Did you fall for his charm without considering his true nature? It's easy to be swept away by his enthusiasm, but it could be too much to handle in the long run. Forget trying to change this man. He will always run his own show. You'll either have to adjust to his lifestyle and temperament or find someone else. A relationship that is built on a fantasy will never yield happiness. It might be a good idea to do a bit of soul searching before you make any commitments.

Thoughts...
Don't let differences discourage you. Differences may be the glue that holds a relationship together - provided you inspire each other. View the challenges from a constructive perspective.

THE FEMALE

YOUR DATE: ARIES
21 March–20 April

The Essence of her

Energetic and enthusiastic – assertive in every aspect of her life – intelligent – strong, independent and confident – has a low tolerance for weakness, but defends those who do not have her strength – a good friend – enjoys a challenge, both professionally and personally – charming – lively – body-conscious and attractive –efficient; hates wasting time

...and remember: Don't be fooled by her pleasant and warm personality – this woman won't settle for a quiet life. The moment things start slowing down is when she will move on and make the next thing happen. Fasten your seatbelt.

Blind Date – speedy essentials

Who's waiting for you?

You'll probably get there at the same time she does. She'll be dashing out of a taxi with a big smile, telling you she had to finish painting her living room or finish a 100-page project – and 'Oh, by the way, where are we going from here?' She is direct and confident, and she will dazzle you with her charm and assertiveness. This energy will set the tone for the evening. If you'd planned an intimate dinner at a romantic bistro, you'd better rethink your agenda. As soon as you've recovered from the energetic hello, you'll notice her attractiveness... This is a very exciting woman.

Emergency fixes for embarrassing pauses.

Embarrassing pauses? These will occur for one of two reasons: either you are absolutely stunning, a Mr Universe who has rendered her speechless (this is virtually impossible), or you have failed to capture her interest (this is more likely). Don't worry. Her dates don't usually get this far. She will make an excuse and be off if she realises it's not a good match. On the other hand, if she likes you and suspects that you're the strong and silent type, your best bet is to be just that. Approach her with intelligent questions, but don't be too serious.

Your place or mine?

Either – or anywhere, for that matter. She is open to erotic adventures. She is also sexually assertive, and she won't wait for a man to make a move. If the chemistry is right and she finds her date attractive – strong, masculine and confident with a good body – moving from A to B comes naturally to her. Although she may be looking for a committed relationship, she doesn't mind if the date turns out to be a one-night stand.

Checklist, before you dash out to meet her:

Display something masculine and personal
(hint: something that has a story)
Prepare several options for how to spend the evening
(hint: make it exciting)
Make sure your wallet is full
(hint: take charge and pick up the bill)
Wear stylish attire that indicates a touch of success
(hint: an expensive shirt, watch or jacket, etc.)
Keep your cellphone turned on
(hint: let her see that you're an active guy)

Tip: She admires strength and masculinity – but if you try to impress her, keep it casual. 'This little scar? Oh, no big deal. I got it when … [fill in the blank with your most gutsy activity]'.

CHAPTER 1

PREPARE YOURSELF

Catch her eye, capture her attention
Top 10 attention grabbers

1. Be playful and tease her a little.
2. Wear something that shows off your masculinity. A t-shirt from an outdoor race or event would be an added bonus.
3. Be confident but a little reserved. Keep her guessing about your interest.
4. Let her see you surrounded by women before you divert your attention to her.
5. Good looks and nice attire are important.
6. Surprise her with one rose – not a dozen.
7. Make your date night active; a concert etc – rather than passive; watching a movie
8. Chose the restaurant based on the atmosphere and energy.
9. Be impulsive. Do something fun on the spur of the moment.
10. Embrace challenges with positivity.

The HE. The man!

The Aries woman can become completely absorbed by a strong and confident guy, especially if he seems disinterested! She'll treat a man who's not yet dazzled by her like a challenge. However, she does prefer attentive guys – strong attentive guys. She may fall for a macho guy, but her interest won't last unless he lives up to her expectations of sensitivity. Her perfect partner is independent, adventurous, ambitious and sensual. Most importantly, he must be able to keep up with her.

The Essence of him
Confident and strong – has a playful gleam in his eyes – physically active: the more adventurous, the better – energetic – ambitious – erotically impulsive – good-looking – loyal and supportive – independent and liberated, but faithful – has a good sense of humour – smart, but never patronising – positive and enthusiastic

Aries arousal meter
From 0 to 100... In five minutes, unless she's already off somewhere. She is easily turned on and doesn't mind giving into erotic feelings anytime and anywhere – well, almost. Scheduling sex is completely out of the question.

Remember: Be true to yourself

It doesn't matter if she is the most stunning girl you've ever met – if you don't match, you don't match. You may be able to put on a show for a while to hold her attention, but what's the point? We can't please everybody. We all have different needs, dreams, tastes and preferences. There's no such thing as a one-size-fits-all lover. Be yourself, and be true to who you are – always!

Very important: It's important to keep up her pace. Kicking back after work is seldom – or never – an option. Her energy is amazing. She will line up activities and expect you to tag along. If you're really not up for it, tell her straight.

CHAPTER 2

THE FIRST DATE

Getting your foot in the door
The basics

Keep it exciting. She loves trying new things. Take her to new places and introduce her to interesting people and exciting activities. Go ahead and suggest things that are a little out of the ordinary. The female Aries can be a daredevil and will love it if you have exciting ideas.

Step on it! ...or step aside. She dislikes boring people and will quickly shake you off if you can't keep up with her. If you want to capture her, fasten your seatbelt and step on it.

Display your masculinity. She is attracted to the strength in a man. If you want to win her heart – or get her into your bed – then draw attention to your masculine side. You won't capture her interest by being soft, gentle and ultra-understanding.

Flex your mind-muscle. A macho attitude alone won't do it. Intelligence, humour and ambition are also important.

Attention and admiration. Don't forget to admire her, desire her and pay her compliments.

Whatever you do...

- **DON'T** feel sorry for yourself.

- **DON'T** be indecisive and ask her to make all the decisions.

- **DON'T** be pessimistic and constantly worry about the future.

- **DON'T** emphasise your allergies, aversions, etc.

- **DON'T** be too obvious about your interest.

Remember, never confuse sex with romance. A physical encounter with an Aries woman doesn't mean you have stirred her deeper emotions.

• **DON'T** be too flashy in an attempt to impress her.

• **DON'T** be reluctant to have sex in unusual places.

• **DON'T** tell her that you prefer going go to bed early enough to

get eight hours sleep every night.

• **DON'T** imply that women are not cut out for male professions.

• **DON'T** plan *everything*.

She doesn't mind entering into a casual relationship that's based only on friendship and sex.

Signs you're in - or not

If you've caught her eye, there will be plenty of signs. She will chase you, play with you, tease you – and then pull back to see if you're still interested. The challenge is to determine the depth and seriousness of her interest. She may regard you as a possible partner – or just see you as a fun lover. These are some signs that her intentions may be more serious:

Chances are she will...

- approach you and invite you out
- pay attention to the things you're interested in
- make you feel special and desired
- surprise you with fun text messages
- suggest that you join her and some friends for a weekend away
- hint at erotic interest

Not your type? Making an exit

It's unlikely that you'll ever find yourself stuck in a relationship with an Aries. She has no time for men or relationships that don't inspire her – and if you're not too keen on her, yours will qualify. She believes that life is for living and exploring – not wasting time on a clueless guy who doesn't appreciate adventure. She may be too busy to notice at first, but as soon as reality hits her, she'll be off.

There are always exceptions to this rule, although they're rare. If your Aries insists on sticking it out with you, you might need to be firmer. She will probably be confused at first, and as soon as she realises that you're serious, she'll get mad. At this point, there's no turning back.

Foolproof exit measures:

Before you try any of these, be prepared to take cover – and don't come out until she's left. They will infuriate her.

- Tell her to lose weight
- Criticise her 'tacky' underwear – no matter how delicate or classy it might be
- Act indifferent about sex and display little or no enthusiasm for it
- Flirt with other women, and pretend not to notice when she gives you the eye
- Demand that she be more submissive
- Insist on knowing everything she's up to

CHAPTER 3

SEX'N STUFF

Seductive moves:
How to get her in the mood:

She is attracted to strong men who can introduce her to new worlds of erotic pleasures, but she doesn't need you to be exotic about it. She's not into Tantric sex or the Kama Sutra. That kind of slow, careful attention to positions would drive her nuts. She has no patience for elaborate lovemaking. Something simple, juicy and a little sassy is enough to spark her interest – and her passion.

Preferences and erotic nature

Sex with an Aries woman must always be a mutual thing. If you expect her to live out her creative side, you must do your bit as well. She is ruled by energy, and her need for adventure applies to her erotic life, too. She'll tingle with excitement about anything out of the ordinary. Visuals, either still or live, can be very arousing for her. If you decide to try role playing, never opt to take the passive part. She doesn't like passive guys – even if it's just an act.

Hitting the right buttons

Although every sign has areas on the body that are more sensitive than others, individual sensitivity may vary quite a bit. Don't go body-blind. Honing in on these erogenous zones and forgetting the rest of her is not a good idea. Use these areas to create sparks while turning her on, and as a passion-booster when things get heated. Watch her body language – including the most obvious of signs. Open your mind to the sensuality of touch and taste.

Key areas
Her face, forehead, scalp and ears

Get it on
Whenever you want to whisper something to her, make sure to brush gently against her ear with your tongue or lips. Although it may not seem like much to you, this contact produces tiny tingles all over her body.

Arouse her
In addition to her ears, pay close attention to her face and scalp. Careful, light touches with your fingertips across her face can have a magic effect. Light kisses in these areas will give her goosebumps. But fair warning: don't start playing around with these erogenous zones unless you're serious about having sex. As soon as you've managed to turn her on, she'll expect you to deliver.

Surprise her

Pull her close, tell her how beautiful she is and how much you want her, gently bite her earlobe – and let her go. Turn around and start doing something completely different. It won't be long before she touches your shoulder and asks you if there's anything else on your mind…

Spice it up

Set the alarm clock a little earlier than usual and surprise her in the shower. You can also give her an exotic gift: an erotic toy, an aromatic oil or sexy underwear.

Remember: No matter how tired and uninspired you may be, never act indifferent while having sex with her. If you're not feeling up to it, it's better to let her know and save it for another time.

Her expectations

Be assertive. Be erotic. Be fun! Her preferences in bed? Easy! She likes anything that is fun, exciting and adventurous. She expects her partner to be assertive and sensual. If he can impress her with erotic creativity, she'll probably put him on speed dial.

Admiration and desire. Her partner needs to compliment her body and her lacy underwear, especially if she gives him a private striptease. She's confident in her body and enjoys showing it off. She knows exactly how to move in order to excite her partner...

Don't linger too long. Although she thinks foreplay is nice, she prefers to move on to the main course pretty quickly. Fiddling about with her erogenous zones for too long can make her restless. She wants and needs a strong partner who's able to satisfy her craving for playful and passionate sex.

Show some energy. She is an assertive sexual partner and tends to take command in bed. However, that doesn't mean her man can just lie back and enjoy it. He needs to make an effort to please her – and if he doesn't, he'll be out of her bed very quickly.

Your sensual preferences
Quiz yourself and find out whether this woman is for you.

Where on the scale are you?
1 = Don't agree | 3 = Sure | 5 = Agree!

1. If the erotic mood is right, the 'when' and 'where' don't really matter.
One a scale for 1 to 5, you are: 1 - 2 - 3- 4 - 5

2. Attention to your partner's body is important, both before and during sex.
One a scale for 1 to 5, you are: 1 - 2 - 3- 4 - 5

3. It's essential that a woman is as passionate and assertive as her man.
One a scale for 1 to 5, you are: 1 - 2 - 3- 4 - 5

4. New experiences should be the rule, not the exception – provided they feel natural and fun.
One a scale for 1 to 5, you are: 1 - 2 - 3- 4 - 5

Score.
15 - 20: This is a passionate union... If the mood is right, you'll probably try to squeeze in several erotic moments each day.
10 - 14: She probably knocked your socks off the first time you spent the night together ... and you have probably been addicted since then.
5 - 9: She may be a little too much at times, but the pleasure keeps you buzzing.
1 - 4: This could be a challenge. If you don't communicate your needs and preferences, she may run over you.

CHAPTER 4

GENERAL STUFF

The big picture

Keep in mind that the characteristics of a Aries may vary quite a bit depending on where within the sign she was born, as well as a wide range of additional astrological factors. But for now, let's stick to the basics. Just remember: don't jump to conclusions as soon as you meet her. Give her room to shine. Get to know the woman behind the sign.

Her personality: Pros and cons

Pros	Cons
• Enthusiastic	• Arrogant
• Energetic and lively	• Cynical
• Efficient	• Dislikes weakness
• Assertive	• Snobbish
• Intelligent, with a sharp mind	• Aggressive
• Independent	• Impatient
• Confident and courageous	• Ignorant
• Feminine and attractive	• Pushy
• Charming	• Possessive
• Adventurous	• Insensitive
• Responsible	• Superficial
• Interesting and engaging	• Romantically restless
• A loyal friend	• Vain
• Passionate	• Obsessed with the chase

Tip: How to show romantic interest

Romance with an Aries woman will always be based on adventure and mutual interests. Gifts, chocolate and flowers are out. Invite her along for something dynamic and fun: a rafting trip, a local wine tasting, etc.

Romantic Vibes

Miss Aries:
The energetic and inspiring partner

The essence

Why wait? She is determined when it comes to romance, and she doesn't mind taking the initiative – in fact, it's natural for her. She is very goal-oriented, so she'll never sit around and wait for a guy to make a move.

Teasing and chasing. An Aries woman can make a suitor go slightly crazy. She may clown around, be charming and attentive and make him feel like he's the most interesting man in the world – and then suddenly pull back and play hard to get. It may sound a little mean, but that's not her intention. She simply loves the chase – and the male attention.

A little bit of both... Although she may fantasise about a macho guy, deep down, she longs for a gentleman who woos her with love and loyalty.

***My* man!** If she has fallen for someone, she will approach him directly and push all female competition aside. Some men may find this overzealous, but if the guy is scared off by her assertiveness, he's not for her.

Adventurous and fun. When she finally finds her man, she will be an amazing partner. She will take the initiative to experience new things – whether an exotic holiday or simply something fun at home. The relationship will never get old. Life with the female Aries will always be an adventure.

Tip: How to show erotic interest

Be direct. Admire her body. Smile seductively and touch her gently... She is no slow starter, and she will pick up on your hints very quickly.

Erotic Vibrations

Miss Aries:
The passionate and assertive lover

The essence

Spicy erotic menu. Sex and sensuality mean a lot to her, but she doesn't need an all-nighter to feel satisfied. Sometimes a passionate and impulsive quickie is all it takes.

No prude. If the mood turns hot unexpectedly, she may be persuaded to have sex in an unusual place.

Sassy and assertive. If you are used to being in charge – and sexually, literally on top – you should prepare yourself for a surprise or two. The female Aries is an assertive woman who enjoys being in command. However, she's no erotic steamroller. She is feminine and playful.

Passion and presence rule! She is always present in the moment and engaged in her erotic feelings. Men who have experienced this woman sexually will often rate the encounter among their lifetime highlights.

No mixed signals, please. Never mislead the Aries woman. If you have given her the impression that you're ready for sex, then you'd better deliver! If you don't, she will write you off as a hopeless cause.

A sensual firework. She is a dream when it comes to bringing sparkle and adventure to your sex life. Satisfying her partner is just as important to her as her own satisfaction.

CHAPTER 5

COMPATIBILITY QUIZ

Are you banging your head against the wall, or does she unleash your positive potential? Do you provoke her or bring out the best in her? Is she making you throw your arms into the air in exasperation, or do you feel inspired and complete in her company? Take the test to find out.

Question no 1
You've been looking forward to a nice, romantic weekend at home. How do you respond when your partner tells you that she's planned to take you to an erotic exhibition and then to a show?

A - Wow! Great fun!
B - I would appreciate her initiative, but I'd ask her to take one of her friends instead.
C - That's just typical. Whenever I want a quiet weekend, she wants to take off somewhere. This woman is wearing me out!

Question no 2
When do you feel the most intense excitement?

A – When they draw the lucky numbers during the weekly lottery on TV.
B – When engaging in physical activities like skydiving, scuba diving or skiing.
C – During passionate and adventurous sex.

(cont.)

Question no 3
How well do you deal with an independent and ambitious woman?

A – Quite well, provided she's not aggressive or demanding.
B - Not very well. This whole 'independence' thing puts me off. What's wrong with a man being a man and a woman being a woman?
C – Very well. I respect women who are ambitious and achieve their goals.

Question no 4
How would you normally approach a woman you're meeting for the first time?

A – With loads of compliments, even if I don't mean half of what I'm saying.
B – With humour, intelligence and masculinity.
C – With a playful and seductive smile.

Question no 5
The two of you are out having a drink. How would you react if your girlfriend told a woman off for flirting with you?

A – It would be a little embarrassing, but it'd be nice to know that she cares.
B – I wouldn't like that. An innocent flirtation can make the day more exciting.
C – I'd love that. I think it's great when a woman is prepared to tell the world: 'That's my man; lay off!'

Question no 6
Do you ever leave your girlfriend wondering whether you want to have sex or not?

A – Yes – that's a game I love to play.
B - Never! When I feel like having sex, I playfully tell her: 'I want you! I want you now!'
C - Sometimes, but I never intend to tease her.

Question no 7
How do you feel about having a partner who is strong and passionate in bed?

A - That's all I've ever wanted!
B - I dislike dominating women. I would prefer a soft, sensitive, cuddly and romantic partner.
C - I don't mind, provided she gives me the opportunity to dominate her every now and again.

Question no 8
Are you easily aroused?

A - Sometimes. It depends on my mood.
B – Oh, yes.
C - I firmly believe that sex should be planned in advance. The setting needs to be right.

Question no 9
How would you react if your girlfriend surprised you on your birthday by filling your home with cheerful party people?

A – I'm not into surprises – especially surprise parties.
B – I don't know … I'd have mixed feelings, but I'd probably enjoy myself.
C – Great fun!

Question no 10
On a scale from 1 to 10, how impulsive are you?

A – A solid 10. I'm so impulsive it's almost a hassle sometimes.
B - Around a 1 or 2. I find impulsiveness very distracting.
C – Somewhere in the middle. Sometimes I'm impulsive, sometimes I'm not.

SCORE	A	B	C
Question 1	10	5	1
Question 2	1	10	5
Question 3	5	1	10
Question 4	1	10	5
Question 5	5	1	10
Question 6	1	10	5
Question 7	10	1	5
Question 8	5	10	1
Question 9	1	5	10
Question 10	10	1	5

75 – 100

How does it feel to know that you've captured the woman of your dreams? You won't have many boring moments in your life – the Aries woman will see to that! Your sex life will be an adventure, too. You know exactly how to handle her, and she loves it. There is no need to discuss or justify anything. You're on the same level, and you share a basic understanding of what makes life fun and interesting. There is no need to look elsewhere. The person who can make you happiest is right by your side.

51 – 74

As long as you stick with her, you will never be bored. There might be a few passionate arguments, but the occasional thunderstorm always clears the air and leaves the earth fresh and fertile. You feel free around her and can talk to her about anything, including your intimate needs and desires. She is no prude, and she gets a kick out of your juicy ideas. She truly loves strong, intelligent men, so don't hold back on your masculinity – but don't put on a show, either. Be yourself and nurture your ambitions. Take care of this woman – she's going to bring you a lot of happiness.

26 – 50

You may feel torn between two worlds. On one hand, you love your partner's energy, enthusiasm and optimism, and the fact that there's never a challenge too big to overcome. On the other hand, you sometimes feel drained. You wish there was more structure and peace in your life. It all boils down to your feelings, values and aspirations. If you're not clear on what those are, then it might be a good idea to find out. If your love is strong and your values are shared, there ought to be a path you can follow. The worst thing you can do is close your eyes and hope for the best. When you finally open them again, she may already be gone...

10 – 25

Do you ever actually communicate, or are you just shouting at each other? Have you ever tried to understand her needs – truly? Do you feel that she's neglecting your needs, too? You are probably either too bossy or too timid for her taste. It'll take great care to make this relationship work. You'll have to make quite a few sacrifices – and is it really worth it? The female Aries is passionate, fun-loving, ambitious and impulsive – and always on the go. Deep down, you know she's an inspiration and a great source of energy. But can you handle her? And does she have what it takes to make you happy?

Thoughts...
If you don't communicate, you won't be able to set things straight. Never rush to conclusions.

...and finally:

This book has not been approved by your date and should be treated accordingly. He or she may not agree with the content.

www.ingramcontent.com/pod-product-compliance
Lightning Source LLC
Chambersburg PA
CBHW071837020426
42331CB00007B/1767